Argyll and the Highlands' Lost Rai

by

Gordon Stansfield

Engine No. 103 at the closed station of Tomatin
with the 1335 excursion from Inverness to Perth,
30 August 1965.

PICTURE ACKNOWLEDGEMENTS
The publishers wish to thank the following for contributing pictures to this book: Hugh Brodie for the front cover and pages 4, 7, 10, 12, 14, 19, 20, 21, 24, 27, 28, 29, 30, 35, 37, 38, 43, 45, 46 and 47; Richard Casserley for pages 33, 34 and 40; the Rev. D.J. Lane for pages 31 and 32; and W.A.C. Smith for pages 1, 6, 17, 25, 48 and the inside back cover.

An early view of Oban and its station, which is still open, from 1880.

INTRODUCTION

The Scottish Highlands possess some of the most spectacular scenery within the United Kingdom and this is most notable in the five highland counties of Argyll, Caithness, Inverness-shire, Ross and Cromarty, and Sutherland. Bringing the railway to these areas was a tremendous feat, not just in terms of the difficulty of construction through wild terrain, but also in terms of funding the cost of building and operating railway lines in these rural settings.

In many instances the railway came much later to these areas compared to the rest of Scotland. Wick and Thurso in Caithness saw the railway arrive from Inverness in 1874, Oban in Argyll was reached in 1880, and in 1897 Kyle of Lochalsh followed suit when the line from Inverness was opened. The main hub of railway activity was Inverness, known affectionately as the Capital of the Highlands, and was first reached from Perth in 1863. This route ran from Aviemore via Forres, but it was not until 1898 that the most direct route via Carr Bridge, still in use today, was opened.

It is difficult nowadays to appreciate just how important the railways were to the Highlands. At the height of the railway era Argyll had thirty stations, Caithness eighteen, Inverness-shire eighty-one, Ross and Cromarty thirty-eight, and Sutherland sixteen. Today the total is a mere sixty-eight for all the counties. Road transport was virtually non-existent and every village was keen to have its own railway station. The railways brought prosperity, for example by opening up new markets for the fishing fleets of Kyle of Lochalsh and Mallaig, which were able to have their catches arrive in London twelve hours after landing. And for ordinary people the railway created a freedom never experienced before by giving them the opportunity to travel outside of their own areas for the first time.

The main railway operator in the north was the Highland Railway Company, although the Caledonian and North British were prominent in Argyll. Most of the lines were single track with passing places, a factor which posed at times major operating problems especially during the First World War when a considerable number of forces personnel and equipment were shipped from England to serve the fleet at Scapa Flow.

Service levels on most lines were very basic with perhaps just two to three trains a day. There were rarely trains on a Sunday and there were even riots at Strome Ferry in 1883, caused by sabbatarians objecting to fish traffic being moved by rail on a Sunday. The area also saw a few branch lines being constructed with some impressive engineering works such as the Connel Ferry bridge. With the decline in passenger usage in the 1960s some branch lines, such as the Ballachulish and Dornoch branches, disappeared. Some had gone much earlier, such as the Lybster to Wick branch.

Luckily, most of the Argyll and Highland lines have survived. Some stations have been reopened over the years, the most recent being Beauly on the line from Inverness to Dingwall. It is hoped that this book will not only rekindle fond memories of days gone by, but will also show to those who never experienced the railway network at its height just how important a role it played in day to day life in Scotland's far flung corners.

Aviemore Station, which is still open.

Ballachulish – Connel Ferry (Connel Ferry Junction)

Passenger service withdrawn	28 March 1966		*Station closed*	*Date*
Distance	27.75 miles		Duror	28 March 1966
Company	Caledonian		Appin	28 March 1966
			Creagan	28 March 1966
Stations closed	*Date*		Barcaldine Halt	28 March 1966
Ballachulish	28 March 1966		Benderloch	28 March 1966
Ballachulish Ferry	28 March 1966		North Connel	28 March 1966
Kentallen	28 March 1966			

Ballachulish Station was known as 'Ballachulish and Glencoe' until July 1905, then 'Ballachulish (Glencoe) for Kinlochleven' until 1908.

Ballachulish Station.

The Ballachulish branch line was opened to passengers on 24 August 1903 by the Callander & Oban Railway Company, just under five years after the first sod had been cut. The line had two notable bridges – Connel and Creagan. After crossing Connel Bridge from Connel Ferry Station, North Connel Station (opened on 7 March 1904) was reached. The line then continued to Ballachulish, famous for its slate quarries. The bridge at Connel is still in use today, but now carries road traffic.

Kentallan Station, 26 March 1966.

Initially the railway company was strictly opposed to vehicles using the Connel bridge, but in 1909 it introduced a motor charabanc service to North Connel and Benderloch. This was known in the area as the Connel railbus, and consisted of a passenger-carrying motor vehicle modified to run on train tracks. It could even transport cars by having them loaded onto a flat wagon. In 1913, when the threat of a chain ferry service for cars arose, the Caledonian decided that a road could be placed adjacent to the railway line. This opened in 1914 as a vehicle-only toll bridge – pedestrians had to cross by train.

Class 2P 0-4-4T No. 55263 at Duror Station with a train for Oban, 8 August 1959.

The pattern of services on the line in the opening years was five return workings, all of which extended to or from Oban. The last train on a Saturday night was often full of revellers from Oban, and if the Glasgow train was late arriving at Connel Ferry Station many passengers adjourned to the local hotel for a refreshment before being summoned back by a blast on the engine's whistle.

Creagan Station.

In 1953 the line was closed from May to August due to severe flooding. Ballachulish Ferry Station was closed to passengers from 1 January 1917 until 1 March 1919 as a wartime economy measure. Freight services were withdrawn nine months before the line was closed to passengers. The Connel Viaduct is a lasting reminder of this branch line.

Engine No. 55263 with its train for Oban, taking water at Creagan, 8 August 1959.

Benderloch Station.

Banavie Pier – Fort William (Banavie Branch Junction)

Passenger service withdrawn	4 September 1939	*Stations closed*	*Date*
Distance	0.75 miles	Banavie Pier	4 September 1939
Company	North British		

Banavie Pier Station was situated alongside the Caledonian Canal on a spur that branched off the West Highland line extension from Fort William to Mallaig. Trains began using the line on 1 June 1895. The station was initially known as Banavie, but when a station of the same name was opened on the Fort William to Mallaig route it was changed to Banavie Pier. Although this change appeared in railway timetables and other publications, the nameboard at Banavie Pier remained unchanged throughout the station's life. The station was built at a time when the promoters of the West Highland line were hoping for a route to Inverness, although in the event Banavie Pier Station remained a branch terminus until closure. Train services to the pier were sparse. In 1922 one train left Fort William at 11.00 a.m. and arrived at the pier station nine minutes later. The return working was at 3.15 p.m. and the service only ran on Mondays, Wednesdays and Fridays.

Boat of Garten (Boat of Garten Junction) – Craigellachie (Craigellachie Junction) *

Passenger service withdrawn	18 October 1945	*Stations closed*	*Date*
Distance	33.25 miles	Nethy Bridge	18 October 1965
Company	Great North of Scotland	Ballifurth Farm Halt	18 October 1965

Known as the Speyside line, this line began its journey northwards at Boat of Garten alongside the Highland Railway line and ran to Craigellachie where connections could be made to Elgin, Keith and Aberdeen. Passenger services began in 1866. Diesel trains came to the line in 1958 and the following year British Railways decided to open four halts – Imperial Cottages, Gilbey's Cottages, Dalvey Farm and Ballifurth Farm. Following the Beeching Report the Speyside line was closed.

* Closed stations on this line that were in Moray were Grantown on Spey East, Cromdale, Dalvey Farm Halt, Dalvey, Advie, Ballindalloch, Blacksboat, Knockando, Gilbey's Cottages, Knockando House Halt, Imperial Cottages Halt, Carron, and Dailuaine Halt. The closed station in Banffshire was Aberlour.

Campbeltown – Machrihanish

Passenger service withdrawn	November 1931
Distance	6 miles
Company	Campbeltown & Machrihanish Light Railway

Stations closed	Date
Campbeltown	November 1931
Plantation	November 1931
Moss Road	November 1931
Moy Park	June 1912
Lintmill	November 1931
Drumlemble	November 1931
Machrihanish Farm	November 1931
Trodigal	November 1931
Colliery Road	October 1927
Machrihanish	November 1931

An engine and train on Hall Street, Campbeltown.

HALL STREET, CAMPBELTOWN & MACHRIHANISH RAILWAY.

This line ran east to west across the Mull of Kintyre, linking Campbeltown with Machrihanish. The government order approving its construction was issued in February 1905 and the line opened to passenger traffic in August the following year. It was an instant success with 10,000 passengers being carried in the first three weeks. Part of the line followed the route of railways serving local coal mines. Most of the coal mined was used locally with ownership in the hands of the Campbeltown Coal Company.

The Campbeltown & Machrihanish Light Railway's locomotive 'Atlantic' (No. 1098). An 0-6-2T, it was built by Andrew Barclay of Kilmarnock in 1907.

The Campbeltown terminus was situated as close to the arrival points of the steamers as possible. Daily sailings arrived from Glasgow and other Clyde coast resorts and during the summer months the level of this traffic was very high.

Kilkerran Crossing with Campbeltown in the background.

On leaving Campbeltown the railway travelled along the public highway before reaching its dedicated track. There were five to six return journeys on weekdays with additional trains provided as required. The six mile journey took about half an hour.

'Atlantic' at Machrihanish.

By the mid-1920s bus services were competing with the railway, and at one time the railway augmented its service by running its own buses. This competition, coupled with a reduction in the coal traffic and problems with the locomotives used on the service, led to the railway's demise. Services were suspended in November 1931 and the track was quickly dismantled. By 1933 the only remains of this railway were odd bits left by the contractor.

Corrour – Tulloch

Passenger service withdrawn	8 September 1932
Distance	1.5 miles
Company	North British

In the late 1920s and early 1930s there were several hydroelectric generating schemes in the Highlands. One such scheme was in Lochaber where a hydroelectric plant was built to provide power to a factory at Fort William owned by the British Aluminium Company. This involved raising the level of Loch Treig by 33 feet, with the result that this part of the West Highland line was submerged at the north end of the loch.

Corrour Station, which is still in use.

Dornoch – The Mound (The Mound Junction)

Passenger service withdrawn	13 June 1960	*Stations closed*	*Date*
Distance	7.75 miles	Dornoch	13 June 1960
Company	Highland	Embo	13 June 1960
		Skelbo	13 June 1960
		Cambusavie Halt	13 June 1960

The branch line from The Mound to Dornoch was authorised under the Light Railway Act of 1896. Opened to passengers on 2 June 1902, the station at The Mound afforded connections to Wick and Thurso in the north and Inverness in the south. The pattern of services on the line remained unchanged for many years with three return journeys being operated. One unusual service was introduced in the summer of 1906. Operating only on Fridays, it was a named train – 'The Far North Express'. This departed from Inverness Station at 4.30 p.m. and ran non-stop to The Mound before continuing onwards to Dornoch. Strangely there was no corresponding return working and at the end of the summer of 1906 the service was withdrawn. Both freight and passenger services were withdrawn in June 1960. A large number of station closures took place on the line from Inverness to Wick and Thurso at the same time, resulting in the closure of The Mound Station.

16XX 0-6-0PT No. 1649 at Skelbo Station with the 2.50 p.m. service from The Mound to Dornoch, 27 August 1959.

Forres (West Junction) – Aviemore (Aviemore Junction) *

Passenger service withdrawn	18 October 1965	*Stations closed*	*Date*
Distance	35.75 miles	Broomhill	18 October 1965
Company	Highland	Boat of Garten	18 October 1965

Boat of Garten Station.

* Closed stations on this line that were in Moray were Rafford, Dunphail, Dava, Castle Grant Platform, and Grantown on Spey West.

Boat of Garten Station.

Opened on 3 August 1883, this line provided the first through service between Perth and Inverness, joining the Inverness to Aberdeen line at Forres. (In 1898 the shorter route to Inverness from Aviemore via Carr Bridge was opened.) Boat of Garten Station was the junction where services from Craigellachie converged from the Great North of Scotland line, with most continuing south for the last few miles to Aviemore. The line over Dava summit was steeply graded and was prone to severe snowdrifts in the winter months. There were three trains in each direction in 1922, with the journey time being about an hour and a quarter. In 1978 the Strathspey Railway reopened the line from Boat of Garten to Aviemore, thereby introducing steam to this line once again. The station buildings at Boat of Garten have been restored and feature quite regularly in period dramas and films. In more recent years the line has been further extended and now reaches Broomhill where the station has been featured in the BBC drama *Monarch of the Glen*.

Fort Augustus – Spean Bridge (Spean Bridge Junction)

Passenger service withdrawn	1 December 1933	*Stations closed*	*Date*
Distance	23.25 miles	Fort Augustus	1 December 1933
Company	North British	Aberchalder	1 December 1933
		Invergarry	1 December 1933
		Invergloy	1 December 1933
		Gairlochy	1 December 1933

Engine No. 48 at Fort Augustus, *c.*1906.

Although the Fort Augustus to Spean Bridge line ended up as a branch line, it might have reached Inverness if events had taken a different turn. Inverness was the territory of the Highland Railway, but the North British hoped that it could make an inroad in some way. The Invergarry & Fort Augustus Railway Company, who were the first owners of the line, were looked upon by the North British as holding the key to reaching Inverness. The line had cost them a lot of money to build with the result that when it was completed in 1901 there were no funds left to purchase any rolling stock in order to operate it. The North British were approached to see if they wished to operate it, but their terms were not accepted. Instead the Highland Railway Company were invited to make an offer. They were keen to get involved as they wished to make an inroad into North British territory at Fort William, a prospect which alarmed their rivals. A stramash ensued, the outcome of which was that the Highland were empowered to work the line in 1903 with the stipulation that they made no attempt to reach Fort William; likewise the North British agreed to drop plans to reach Inverness. In 1907 the Highland withdrew from operating the line and the North British took over in 1921. Revenue on the line became so low that services were withdrawn in October 1911 and not restored until 1 August 1913. In 1914 the North British bought the line. When the London & North Eastern Railway took it over they continued passenger services until 1933 and freight services until 1946.

A 4-4-0 locomotive, No. 55, at Fort Augustus Station, 1914.

Fort Augustus Pier – Fort Augustus

Passenger service withdrawn	1 October 1906	*Station closed*	*Date*
Distance	1 mile	Fort Augustus Pier	1 October 1906
Company	Highland		

Situated to the south of Loch Ness, this was a short extension to the Invergarry and Fort Augustus Railway Company's line from Spean Bridge to Fort Augustus. The line was opened right through to Fort Augustus Pier in 1903 and was operated by the Highland Railway. Trains to the pier only ran during the summer months, and although the line was fairly short it had a hand-operated swing bridge over the Caledonian Canal and a viaduct over the River Onich. At the pier station passengers could board a boat for a trip on Loch Ness. In 1905 the Highland Railway applied to operate their own steamer service on Loch Ness and the Caledonian Canal, thereby providing a service between Fort Augustus and Inverness. At that time Government approval was required and the Highland met stiff opposition from David McBrayne Ltd, resulting in the proposal being shelved. The passenger service to Fort Augustus pier lasted just three years. However, a goods service continued until July 1924 after which the pier was demolished, the rails lifted and the swing bridge over the canal fixed open permanently.

Fort George – Gollanfield Junction

Passenger service withdrawn	5 April 1943	Station closed	Date
Distance	1.5 miles	Fort George	5 April 1943
Company	Highland		

Fort George Station.

This branch off the Inverness to Aberdeen line was opened on 1 July 1899. The station where it left the main line was initially called Fort George, but had its name changed to Gollanfield Junction upon the opening of the line. Although the terminus was called Fort George it was actually in the village of Arderseir. In 1922 there were ten return journeys to and from Gollanfield Junction, most of which allowed for connections to Nairn and Inverness. Passenger services were withdrawn in 1943, but military trains continued to run to Fort George, which was a manned garrison. Freight traffic continued along the branch until August 1958.

Fortrose – Muir of Ord (Muir of Ord Junction)

Passenger service withdrawn	1 October 1951	*Stations closed*	*Date*
Distance	13.5 miles	Fortrose	1 October 1951
Company	Highland	Avoch	1 October 1951
		Munlochy	1 October 1951
		Allangrange	1 October 1951
		Redcastle	1 October 1951

Fortrose Station.

Fortrose Station.

This branch line was opened on 1 February 1894. It ran through the Black Isle and consequently became known as the Black Isle line. Parliamentary powers were obtained to extend the branch two and a quarter miles beyond Fortrose to Rosemarkie, but this was never done. Bradshaw's 1922 edition showed three return workings on weekdays, all of which connected with trains to and from Inverness and Wick/Thurso at Muir of Ord Station. By 1949 there were only two return journeys on weekdays, with three workings to Fortrose and four to Muir of Ord on Saturdays. Freight services continued on the line until June 1960, and although Muir of Ord Station closed on 13 June 1960 it was subsequently reopened on 4 October 1976.

Class 3F 0-6-0 No. 57594 at Avoch with the Fortrose branch freight, 25 August 1959.

Munlochy Station.

Fort William (first station) – Fort William

Passenger service withdrawn	9 June 1975	*Station closed*	*Date*
Distance	0.5 miles	Fort William (first station)	9 June 1975
Company	North British		

Fort William Station.

Fort William Station.

In the mid-1970s improvements were made to Fort William town centre. There was severe traffic congestion, especially during the summer months, and to alleviate this the decision was made to build a bypass. The railway and bus station, including the bus garage which had been used by McBrayne's, were relocated to the eastern end of the town. New facilities were built for both, including a bus garage for the then operator, Highland Omnibuses Ltd, on an industrial estate just outside the town. The relocated station is still in use today. During the summer months a steam-hauled service, 'The Jacobite', runs to Mallaig and has been featured in the Harry Potter films as the 'Hogwart's Express'.

4-4-0 No. 227, built at Cowlairs in 1896, at Fort William.

4-4-0 No. 364 at Fort William, 24 July 1913.

Fort William (Loch Linnhe Pier) – Lochaber (Aluminium Smelter Factory)

Passenger service withdrawn	1930s	*Stations closed*	*Date*
Distance	2 miles	Fort William (Loch Linnhe Pier)	1930s
Company	British Aluminium Factory	Lochaber (Aluminium Smelter Factory)	1930s

This line was constructed in 1925 when work began on the Lochaber aluminium smelter factory. It started at a pier on Loch Linnhe and after two miles reached a camp adjacent to where the factory was being built. The line's gauge was three feet and it carried men and materials to the factory. It then ran a further 19 miles to Loch Treig where a dam was being constructed in connection with a hydroelectric scheme. The main passenger service was at weekends when workers engaged on the various projects would travel to and from Fort William. The railway remained in use for freight traffic until the 1960s and by 1971 the track had been lifted.

Inverness Harbour – Inverness (Harbour Branch Junction)

Passenger service withdrawn	June 1897	*Station closed*	*Date*
Distance	0.75 miles	Inverness Harbour	June 1897
Company	Highland		

The Inverness Harbour branch opened to passengers in November 1855 and provided a service from Inverness Station to the harbour to connect with steamer services. These did not prove to be very popular and the service was subsequently withdrawn.

Inverness Station, 1957. This station is still open.

Engine No. 1646 shunting at Inverness Station, June 1961. Diesel locomotive No. 5130 is shunting up the postal train.

Kinlochleven (Aluminium Smelter Factory) – Blackwater Reservoir

Passenger service withdrawn	1929	*Stations closed*	*Date*
Distance	2 miles	Kinlochleven (Aluminium Smelter Factory)	1929
Company	British Aluminium Company	Loch Leven Wharf	1929
		Blackwater Reservoir	1929

This line was built to serve the British Aluminium Company's smelter factory at Kinlochleven. Opened in stages between 1907 and 1911, it was the forerunner to a second line which was later built at Lochaber to serve a smelter factory. The electrified line had a gauge of three feet and ran to the factory from a wharf at the loch side to the factory and then to Blackwater Reservoir set among the hills above Kinlochleven. A limited number of passengers were carried in connection with works traffic. In 1989 plans were put forward to relay the line as a tourist attraction, but these were subsequently dropped.

Lochaber (Aluminium Smelter Factory) – Loch Treig

Passenger service withdrawn	1929	*Stations closed*	*Date*
Distance	19 miles	Loch Treig	1929
Company	British Aluminium Company		

This line ran from Loch Treig to the base camp at the aluminium smelter factory at Lochaber where another section of line continued to Fort William. It had a gauge of three feet and carried passengers as well as construction materials. At weekends as many as 300 workmen travelled along the line, which remained in use until the smelter was completed.

Lochluichart Deviation

			Date
Passenger service withdrawn	3 May 1954	Stations closed	
Distance	2 miles	Lochluichart (first station)	3 May 1954
Company	Highland		

The Lochluichart Deviation involved the construction of a two mile detour on the line between Dingwall and Kyle of Lochalsh. This was required because of a hydroelectric scheme and involved the building of a new bridge over the River Conon, as well as new rock cuttings and embankments. The original Lochluichart Station had to be resited as the scheme involved raising the loch level. This was one of two hydroelectric schemes in the Highlands which required line deviation – the other being at Loch Treig on the West Highland line between Corrour and Tulloch.

Lybster – Wick (Wick Junction)

		Station closed	Date
Passenger service withdrawn	1 April 1944	Occumster	1 April 1944
Distance	13.75 miles	Roster Road Halt	1 April 1944
Company	Highland	Mid Clyth	1 April 1944
		Ulbster	1 April 1944
Stations closed	Date	Welsh's Crossing Halt	1 April 1944
Lybster	1 April 1944	Thrumster	1 April 1944
Parkside Halt	1 April 1944		

The Wick & Lybster Light Railway was opened in 1903 and was one of the few railways to receive financial assistance from the government, with the Treasury providing a grant of £25,000 towards its construction. The Highland Railway agreed to operate the line as it knew it would acquire traffic – mainly carrying fish from the port of Lybster – which would then travel over its line from Wick to Inverness. The line ran directly south from Wick and in 1908 was included in the area covered by the fortnightly passes sold by the Highland. These gave unlimited travel north of Perth for the sum of £3 for first class travel and £2 for third. To try and stimulate traffic the London, Midland & Scottish Railway opened halts at Parkside, Roster Road and Welsh's Crossing in January 1936. Passing loops were provided at all stations except Thrumster, Ulbster, Mid Clyth and Occumster. When the passenger service was withdrawn in 1944 the line closed completely.

Lybster Station, 1912.

Strathpeffer – Dingwall (Fodderty Junction)

Passenger service withdrawn	23 February 1946	*Station closed*	*Date*
Distance	2.5 miles	Strathpeffer	23 February 1946
Company	Highland		

Strathpeffer Station, 18 May 1928.

If the construction of the railway from Dingwall to Kyle of Lochalsh had gone according to plan, Strathpeffer would have been located on the line and not ended up being served by a branch line. In the event difficulties negotiating with local landowners led to the change of plan. Strathpeffer had become very important as a spa resort and the Highland managed to construct a short branch from Fodderty Junction on the Kyle line. This opened to passenger traffic on 3 June 1885. Following the example of other railway operators elsewhere the Highland opened a hotel at Strathpeffer in June 1911 and, to encourage traffic, ran a through train from Aviemore which passed Inverness without stopping. There was no return working and the express was withdrawn in 1915. Passenger services lingered on until 1946 and freight services lasted until 1951. The station at Strathpeffer was a grand affair and remains in use today as a tourist information centre.

Closed passenger stations on lines still open to passenger services

Line/Service	**Fort William – Crianlarich**	Station closed	Date
		Fersit Halt	1 January 1935
		Auchallander Platform	After 1930
		Gorton	Not known

Line/Service	**Greenhill Upper Junction – Inverness ***	Station closed	Date
		Moy	3 May 1965
Station closed	Date	Daviot	3 May 1965
Kincraig	18 October 1965	Culloden Moor	3 May 1965
Tomatin	3 May 1965		

Kincraig Station was known as 'Boat of Inch' until 1 September 1871.

* Closed stations on this line that were in Stirlingshire were Plean, Bannockburn, and Bridge of Allan. Closed stations in Perthshire were Kinbuck, Greenloaning, Blackford, Auchterarder, Dunning, Forteviot, Forgandenny, Glasgow Road (Perth), Luncarty, Strathord, Stanley, Murthly, Rohallion, Dalguise, Guay, Ballinluig, Killiecrankie, Black Island Platform, Struan, and Dalnaspidal.

Gollanfield Station, 24 August 1938. This station was known as 'Fort George' until 1 July 1899 and 'Gollanfield Junction' until March 1959.

* Closed stations on this line that were in Nairnshire were Kildrummie (previously known as Cawdor) and Auldearn. Closed stations in Moray were Brodie, Kinloss (first), Kinloss (second), Kinloss (third), Alves, Mosstowie, Lhanbryde, Orbliston, Orton, Mulben, and Tauchers Halt. The closed station in Banffshire was Grange. The closed stations in Aberdeenshire were Cairnie Junction, Rothiemay, Gartly, Kennethmont, Wardhouse, Buchanstone, Dyne, Pitcaple, Inveramsey, Inverurie (first), Kintore, Kinaldie, Pitmedden, Dyce (first), Dyce (second), Stoneywood, Bankhead, Bucksburn, Persley Halt, Woodside, Don Street, Kittybrewster, Hutchieson Street, and Schoolhill.

** Known as Culloden until 30 October 1898.

Line/Service	**Kyle of Lochalsh – Dingwall**

Station closed	Date
Duncraig *	7 December 1964
Glencarron **	7 December 1964
Achterneed ***	7 December 1964

* A private platform until 23 May 1949. Renamed Duncraig Platform on 10 September 1962. The name reverted to Duncraig after reopening on 5 January 1976 with trains calling on request.

** Known as Glencarron Platform until 10 September 1962. Unadvertised station.

*** Known as Strathpeffer until 1 June 1885. Reopened on 8 February 1965. After reopening was an unstaffed private halt.

Line/Service	**Oban – Crianlarich (Crianlarich Junction)**

Station closed	Date
Falls of Cruachan Halt *	1 November 1965

Station closed	Date
Ach-Na-Cloich **	1 November 1965
Loch Awe	28 September 1965
Tyndrum (first)	1 May 1877

* Reopened on 20 June 1988 as Falls of Cruachan (open only during the summer months).

** Closed from 1 January 1917 until 1 March 1919.

Loch Awe Station. This reopened on 10 May 1985.

Caledonian Railway 4-6-0 No. 56 with an 8.00 a.m. service from Glasgow (Buchanan Street) to Oban at Loch Awe, 11 July 1929.

Line/Service	Thurso – Georgemas Junction	Station closed	Date
		Hoy	29 September 1965

Line/service	Wick – Inverness		Station closed	Date
			West Helmsdale	19 June 1871
Station closed	Date		Loth	13 June 1960
Bilbster	13 June 1960		Dunrobin Halt **	29 November 1965
Watten	13 June 1960		The Mound	13 June 1960
Bower	13 June 1960		Rogart ***	13 June 1960
Halkirk	13 June 1960		Mid Fearn	1 September 1865
Borrobol *	29 November 1965		Edderton	13 June 1960
Salzcraggie	29 November 1965			

Passengers waiting at Helmsdale Station, which is still open on the line from Wick to Inverness.

* Known as Borrobol Platform until 10 September 1962.
** Reopened on 30 June 1985 as Dunrobin (open only during the summer months).

*** Reopened on 6 March 1961.

Line/service		Station closed	Date
		Foulis	13 June 1960
Station closed	Date	Conon	13 June 1960
Meikle Ferry	1 January 1869	Muir of Ord	13 June 1960
Nigg	13 June 1960	Beauly	13 June 1960
Kildary *	13 June 1960	Clunes	13 June 1960
Delny	13 June 1960	Lentran	13 June 1960
Alness **	13 June 1960	Bunchrew	13 June 1960
Evanton ***	13 June 1960	Clachnaharry	1 April 1913

Wick – Inverness (continued)

Class 5 4-6-0 No. 45479 at The Mound with the 8.25 a.m. service from Wick to Inverness.

* Known as Parkhill until 1 May 1868.   ** Reopened on 7 May 1973.   *** Known as Novar until 31 May 1937.

Bonar Bridge Station, which is still open.

Edderton Station.

Invergordon Station, which is still open.

Muir Of Ord Station was reopened on 4 October 1976.

Muir of Ord Station

Railway Station, Beauly.

Clunes Station, looking east, 25 August 1959.